WHO EATS WHAT?
IN THE FOREST

ROBBIE BYERLY
KATIE AXT

This is a forest.

There are plants in the forest.

ant

bird

snake

frog

mouse

big cat

fish

bug

There are animals in the forest.

The animals have to eat to live.

But who eats what?

This is a plant.

The bug eats the plant.

The frog eats the bug.

The snake eats the frog.

mouse

bird

bug

Who eats the snake?

The bird eats the snake.

This is a plant.

The mouse eats the plant.

The snake eats the mouse.

The bird eats the snake.

frog

fish

big cat

Who eats the bird?

The big cat eats the bird.

This is a plant.

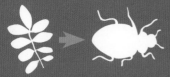

The bug eats the plant.

The fish eats the bug.

The bird eats the fish.

The big cat eats the bird.

elk

wild boar

turkey

deer

moose

mouse

raccoon

coyote

hare

The big cat eats lots of animals.

Who eats the big cat?

No one eats the big cat.

FOREST FOOD WEB

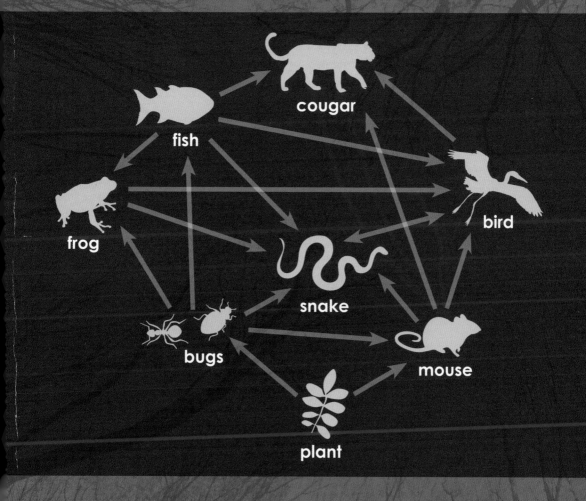

cougar

fish

frog

bird

snake

bugs

mouse

plant

THIS IS HOW
ENERGY FLOWS

FOREST FACTS

 Plants in the forest include ferns, wild flowers, moss, berries, and trees.

 Bugs, such as the longhorn beetle, eat leaves, flowers, fruit, and tree bark.

 Ants eat mostly plants and fruits in the forest.

 Frogs eat bugs such as ants, flies, worms, and spiders.

 Snakes eat frogs, mice, small birds, small mammals, and bugs.

 Fish, such as trout, swim in streams in the forest and eat tiny fish and insects.

 Birds, such as the blue heron, eat snakes, frogs, fish, bugs, and plants.

 Mice eat plants, fruit, seeds, and small bugs.

 Cougars are great hunters and eat birds, deer, elk, coyotes, rabbits, wild boars, mice, raccoons, turkeys, and other animals in the forest.